British Holiday Cookery

Liz Garnett

Beechthorpe Press

First published in 2020 by Beechthorpe Press

ISBN: 978-0-9935603-7-8

CONTENTS

Notes for the reader

Camping and self-catering holidays give you the opportunity to explore the range of local produce on offer and a chance to support the local community. Britain has a thriving local economy of producers selling direct to the public or through farmers markets, farm shops as well as and food box schemes. These include cheeses, meats, fruit and vegetables, ciders, wines and beer.

In order to take as few utensils as possible most ingredients are measured using measuring spoons or measuring cups. Where measurements are in grams it is assumed that these will be measured at the market or supermarket.

SALADS

Salad Dressings

Oil and Vinegar
2 tbsps olive oil
1 tbsp balsamic vinegar

Salad Dressing
2 tbsps olive oil
1 tsp Dijon mustard
1 tbsp balsamic vinegar

Chilli Salad Dressing
2 tbsps olive oil
1 tsp Dijon mustard
1 tbsp lime juice
1 tsp honey
1 small chilli, finely chopped

Honey and Lemon Vinaigrette
1 tbsp lemon juice
1 tbsp honey
2 tbsps olive oil

Garlic Mayonnaise
1 clove garlic, crushed
Juice of 1 lemon
4 tbsps mayonnaise

Paprika Mayonnaise
8 tbsps mayonnaise
½ tsp smoke paprika

Spinach, Bacon and Goats Cheese Salad

Serves 2

Ingredients
2 handfuls spinach, washed
100g streaky bacon, chopped
Handful pine nuts
50g goats cheese, crumbled

Dressing
2 tbsp olive oil
1 tbsp red wine vinegar
Salt and pepper

Instructions
- Place spinach on each plate.
- Dry fry pine nuts until golden brown and sprinkle on spinach.
- Dry fry bacon until well cooked and sprinkle on spinach.
- Crumble goats cheese on spinach.
- Mix dressing and pour over salad.
- Serve with fresh bread.

Scallop and Bacon Salad

Serves 2

Ingredients
30g pack of rocket, washed
8 large scallops
100g streaky bacon, chopped
1 bunch of tarragon, chopped

Dressing
1 tbsp white wine vinegar
2 tbsps olive oil

Instructions
- Place rocket on plates.
- Fry bacon until crispy and remove from heat.
- Add scallops and cook for 2 minutes on each side.
- Place bacon and scallops on top of the rocket.
- Mix the dressing and pour over salad.
- Serve with fresh bread.

Salad Niçoise

Serves 2

Ingredients
½ small cucumber, sliced
2 tomatoes, sliced
2 small artichokes, quartered
½ fennel bulb, very finely sliced
2 spring onions, sliced
1 green pepper, sliced
4 radishes, quartered
2 hard boiled egg, quartered
4 anchovy fillets, rinsed
8 black olives, stoned

Dressing
4 tbsps olive oil
2 cloves garlic, crushed
10 leaves fresh basil, finely chopped
Salt pepper

Instructions
- Arrange salad vegetables, eggs, anchovy fillets, tuna and olives attractively in bowls.
- Mix dressing and pour over salad.
- Serve with fresh bread.

Egg Salad with Asparagus and Bacon

Serves 2

Ingredients
2 hard boiled egg, peeled and sliced
Bunch of asparagus, cooked
100g streaky bacon, chopped and cooked

Dressing
2 tbsps olive oil
1 tbsp balsamic vinegar
1 clove garlic, crushed
1 tsp Dijon mustard

Instructions
- Arrange asparagus on two plates and place egg slices on top of asparagus.
- Mix dressing and pour over asparagus and eggs.
- Sprinkle bacon over eggs and asparagus.
- Serve.

Alternatives
- Replace bacon with chopped smoked salmon pieces.
- Replace bacon with 4 anchovy fillets.

Beetroot Salad with Capers

Serves 2

Ingredients
1 small lettuce
1 medium beetroot, grated raw
3 tbsps capers, chopped
2 tbsps olive oil
2 tbsps lemon juice
75g soft goats cheese, crumbled

Instructions
- Line the bottom of a large bowl with lettuce leaves.
- Combine beetroot, capers, olive oil and lemon juice and pile on top of lettuce.
- Crumble goats cheese on top of beetroot.
- Serve with fresh bread.

Potato Salad with Fennel and Celery

Serves 2

Ingredients
300g new potatoes, thickly sliced
100g streaky bacon
2 sticks celery, finely sliced
1 small bulb fennel, finely sliced

Dressing
1 tbsp lemon juice
1 tbsp olive oil
1 tsp honey

Instructions
- Cook new potatoes until tender.
- Dry fry bacon until crispy. Remove bacon and put to one side.
- Combine potatoes, bacon, celery and fennel.
- Mix lemon juice, olive oil and honey and pour over salad.
- Serve with a selection of cold meats.

Greek Potato Salad

Serves 2

Ingredients
400g new potatoes, halved
1 red pepper, quartered
1 yellow pepper, quartered
4 cherry tomatoes, halved
1 small red onion, sliced
12 pitted black olives
100g feta cheese

Dressing
60ml olive oil
Juice 1 lemon
1 clove garlic, crushed
2 tsps fresh thyme, chopped

Instructions
- Boil potatoes, drain and cool.
- Place peppers skin side down on dry frying pan.
- Cook over a high heat to blacken skins. Remove skins and slice.
- Cut tomatoes in half and combine in bowl with potatoes, peppers, onions, olives and feta.
- Mix dressing and pour over salad.
- Serve with a selection of hams and salamis.

English Potato Salad

Serves 2

Ingredients
300g new potatoes, halved
½ cucumber, cubed
1 little gem lettuce, torn
2 tbsps olive oil
2 tbsps capers
1 tbsp lemon
1 tbsp fresh thyme, finely chopped

Instructions
- Boil potatoes and leave to cool.
- Combine all the ingredients in a bowl and mix well.
- Serve with a selection of cold meats.

Beetroot Coleslaw

Serves 2

Ingredients
1 small carrot, grated
1 small raw beetroot, grated
⅛ red cabbage, finely sliced
1 apple, grated
Handful of pine nuts

Dressing
1 tbsp olive oil
2 tbsps lemon juice
1 tsp honey

Instructions
- Combine ingredients in a large bowl.
- Mix dressing and pour over coleslaw and mix well.
- Serve with a selection of cold meats.

Fennel Coleslaw

Serves 2

Ingredients
1 small bulb fennel, finely sliced
1 green apple, cored and finely sliced
1 carrot, grated
1 stick celery, finely sliced

Dressing
2 tbsps mayonnaise
2 tbsps lemon juice

Instructions
- Combine fennel, apple, carrot, and celery in a bowl.
- Mix dressing and add to the vegetables and stir well.
- Serve with smoked salmon and fresh bread.

Red Cabbage Coleslaw

Serves 2

Ingredients
½ small red cabbage, finely sliced
1 carrot, grated
1 small red onion, finely chopped
½ red chilli, finely chopped

Dressing
2 tbsps mayonnaise
2 tbsps lime juice

Instructions
- Combine cabbage, carrot, onion and chilli in a large bowl.
- Mix dressing and pour the dressing over vegetables and mix well.
- Serve with a selection of cold meats.

Avocado Salad

Serves 2

Ingredients
1 packet rocket
100g streaky bacon, chopped and cooked
1 avocado, sliced
Handful of walnuts or pine nuts

Dressing
2 tbsps balsamic vinegar
1 tbsp olive oil

Instructions
- Place rocket in bowls.
- Add avocado, walnuts and bacon.
- Pour over with dressing.
- Serve with fresh bread.

Lentil Salad with Goats Cheese

Serves 2

Ingredients
1 can green lentils
1 clove garlic, crushed
3 spring onions, sliced
1 red pepper, sliced
2 tomatoes, diced
1 tsp chopped fresh parsley
1 tsp capers

Dressing
1 tbsp olive oil
Juice of 1 lemon
1 tsp Dijon mustard
Salt and pepper
1 oblong soft goats cheese

Instructions
- Rinse lentils and put in a bowl.
- Add pepper, tomatoes, onion, garlic, parsley, and capers.
- Mix dressing and stir into salad.
- Sprinkle crumbled goat cheese on the top.
- Serve with fresh bread.

Prawns and Tomato Salad

Serves 2

Ingredients
2 tbsps olive oil
250g ripe tomatoes, peeled, seeded diced
2 tbsps very finely chopped parsley
2 spring onions, finely sliced
20 large peeled cooked prawns
Parsley to garnish

Dressing
Juice and zest of 1 lime
1 tsp red wine vinegar
1 red chilli, finely chopped
Salt and pepper

Instructions
- Place all ingredients except prawns in a bowl and mix.
- Place tomato salad on plates and place cooked prawns on top.
- Garnish with parsley and pepper.
- Serve with fresh bread.

Tomato Salad

Serves 2

Ingredients
3 tomatoes, sliced
1 small onion, sliced into circles
2 cloves garlic, crushed
Fresh thyme

Dressing
2 tbsps olive oil
1 tbsp vinegar

Instructions
- Arrange tomatoes on a plate with crushed garlic and onions.
- Mix dressing and pour over salad.
- Serve with a selection of cold meats.

Broad Bean Salad

Serves 2

Ingredients
500g broad beans in their pods
50g soft goats cheese, crumbled

Dressing
2 tbsp olive oil
1 tbsp balsamic vinegar
Salt and pepper
1 cup fresh mint, chopped

Instructions
- Shell the beans and add to boiling water.
- Simmer for 3 minutes.
- Drain and refresh in cold water.
- Mix broad beans and crumbled goats cheese.
- Mix dressing and pour over beans and goats cheese.
- Serve with smoked salmon or a selection of cold meats.

Scallop Salad with Red Pepper Dressing

Serves 2

Ingredients
8 large scallops, halved horizontally
1 packet of rocket
1 tbsp capers, rinsed
1 tbsp olive oil

Dressing
½ red pepper, quartered
3 small spring onions, finely sliced
2 small gherkins, finely chopped
1 tbsp freshly parsley, chopped
80ml olive oil
1 tbsp white wine vinegar
Salt and pepper

Instructions
- Arrange rocket leaves and capers on plates.
- Dry fry peppers (skin side down) until well charred.
- Once cooled remove skin and finely chop.
- Mix dressing in a saucepan.
- Place saucepan over a very low heat to warm through.
- Heat 1 tbsp olive oil in a frying pan and add scallops. Cook over a high heat until cooked through.
- Arrange scallops on salad and spoon over warm dressing.
- Serve with fresh bread.

Couscous Salad

Serves 2

Ingredients
½ cup couscous
¾ cup water
8 cherry tomatoes, halved
½ cucumber, diced
4 spring onions, chopped
2 tbsps mint, chopped
3 tbsps parsley, chopped

Dressing
2 tbsps olive oil
2 tbsps lemon juice
Salt and pepper

Instructions
- Boil water and add couscous, cover and leave for 5 minutes.
- Once cooled put couscous, tomatoes, cucumber, spring onions, mint and parsley in a bowl and mix well.
- Mix dressing, pour over salad and mix.
- Serve with a selection of hams or salamis and fresh bread.

Mediterranean Couscous

Serves 2

Ingredients
½ cup couscous
¾ cup boiling water
250g cherry tomatoes, halved
½ cucumber, finely diced
11 radishes, finely sliced
Handful fresh parsley, chopped

Dressing
½ cup Greek yoghurt
2 tbsps lemon juice
1 clove garlic, crushed

Instructions
- Put couscous in a bowl and pour over with boiling water, cover and leave to cool.
- Combine couscous, tomatoes, cucumber, radishes and parsley in a large bowl.
- Mix dressing and pour over salad.
- Mix well.
- Serve with a selection of sliced meats and fresh bread.

Quinoa, Watercress and Goats Cheese Salad

Serves 2

Ingredients
¼ cup quinoa
1 small red onion, finely chopped
1 tbsp olive oil
1 tbsp balsamic vinegar
150g cherry tomatoes, halved
Handful of watercress, torn
10 large green olives, sliced
1 tbsp capers
¼ cup pine nuts
75g firm goats cheese, crumbled

Instructions
- Cook quinoa for 15 minutes in boiling water, drain and leave to cool.
- Combine onion, olive oil, balsamic vinegar, tomatoes, watercress, olives, capers, quinoa and pine nuts in a bowl.
- Mix well.
- Crumble goats cheese on top of salad.
- Serve with sliced ham or smoked salmon and bread.

Quinoa, Avocado and Radish Salad

Serves 2

Ingredients
¼ cup quinoa
1 cup fresh broad beans, cooked
1 small avocado, chopped
Handful radishes, sliced
½ cup fresh basil, chopped

Dressing
2 tbsps lemon juice
2 tbsps olive oil
1 clove garlic, crushed

Instructions
- Cook quinoa for 15 minutes in boiling water, drain and leave to cool.
- Combine quinoa, broad beans, avocado, radishes and basil in a large bowl.
- Mix dressing and pour over salad.
- Serve with a selection of cold meats.

Quinoa and Mozzarella Salad

Serves 2

Ingredients
¼ cup dried quinoa
1 small red onion, finely chopped
½ courgette, finely cubed
4 sundried tomatoes, roughly chopped
1 red pepper, chargrilled and sliced
1 mozzarella, cubed

Dressing
2 tbsps lemon juice
2 tbsps olive oil
1 clove garlic, crushed

Instructions
- Cook quinoa for 15 minutes in boiling water, drain and leave to cool.
- Combine, quinoa, onion, courgette, tomatoes, red pepper and mozzarella in a large bowl.
- Mix dressing and pour over salad.
- Mix well.
- Serve with bread and cold meats.

Quinoa, Prawn and Grapefruit Salad

Serves 2

Ingredients
½ cup quinoa
1 red grapefruit, segmented and reserve juice
1 avocado, sliced
200g prawns, cooked
2 handfuls toasted pine nuts
Handful parsley, chopped

Dressing
2 tbsps olive oil
2 tsps honey
Juice reserved from grapefruit

Instructions
- Cook quinoa in boiling water for 15 minutes, drain and leave to cool.
- Combine quinoa, grapefruit, avocado, prawns, pine nuts and parsley in a bowl.
- Mix dressing and pour over salad.
- Mix well.
- Serve with fresh bread.

ONE POT MEALS

Vegetable Soup

Serves 2

Ingredients
1 tbsp unsalted butter
1 small onion, chopped
1 clove garlic, crushed
1 carrot, sliced
2 celery sticks, sliced
1 leek, sliced
1 courgette, sliced
2 tomatoes, peeled and chopped
500ml water, boiling
Salt and pepper

Instructions
- In a saucepan gently heat onion, garlic, carrot, celery and leeks in butter for 5 minutes over a medium heat.
- Season.
- Add courgette, tomato and boiling water.
- Boil for 5-7 minutes over a high heat until vegetables are just tender.
- Serve with fresh bread.

Vegetable Soup with Chorizo

Serves 2

Ingredients
1 tbsp olive oil
1 onion, chopped
1 clove garlic, crushed
4 tomatoes, peeled and finely chopped
1 carrot, finely chopped
2 sticks celery, sliced
500ml vegetable stock
2 inches of chorizo sausage, thinly sliced

Instructions
- Heat oil in pan and sauté onion for 1 minute.
- Add garlic, tomatoes, carrot, celery, vegetable stock and chorizo.
- Cook over moderate heat for 20 minutes or until the vegetables are cooked.
- Serve with fresh bread.

Clam and Vegetable Soup

Serves 2

Ingredients
2 tbsps olive oil
2 cloves garlic, crushed
1 small red chilli, seeded and chopped
1 small leek, sliced
1 small onion, sliced
1 carrot, finely sliced
1 red pepper, finely sliced
500ml water
24 small clams, well rinsed
1 small bunch of fresh parsley, chopped

Instructions
- Sweat garlic, chilli, leek, onion, carrot and red pepper in oil for 3 minutes.
- Pour in water and simmer for 10 minutes.
- Add clams and boil as quickly as possible until they open.
- Discard any that do not open.
- Pour into bowls and sprinkle with parsley.
- Serve with fresh bread.

Ministrone Soup

Serves 2

Ingredients
1 tbsp olive oil
1 small onion
1 clove garlic, chopped
1 carrot, peeled and diced
2 celery sticks, diced
6 tomatoes, peeled and chopped
600ml water
1 sprig basil, chopped
Salt and pepper
1 can cannelloni beans, drained and rinsed
½ cup soup pasta
Parmesan cheese, freshly grated

Instructions
- Fry onion and garlic, carrot, celery for 2 minutes.
- Add tomatoes, water and basil.
- Season and add beans and simmer gently for 10 minutes.
- Add pasta and simmer until pasta is cooked.
- Pour into bowls and sprinkle with parmesan.
- Serve with fresh bread.

Chicken Soup

Serves 2

Ingredients
Handful of cooked chicken, finely chopped
1 litre chicken stock
1 carrot, cut into matchsticks
1 cake of egg noodles

Instructions
- Heat chicken stock in saucepan.
- Add chicken and carrot.
- Once soup is boiling add noodles and cook until noodles are just soft.
- Serve with fresh bread.

Alternative
- 1 inch of fresh root ginger cut into matchsticks can be added with the chicken and carrot.

Note
- This recipe is ideal if you have any left over chicken from a rotisserie chicken. Alternatively, fry a breast of chicken and finely slice.

Ratatouille

Serves 2

Ingredients
2 tbsps olive oil
1 onion, sliced
1 red pepper, sliced
1 small aubergine, thinly sliced
1 courgette, sliced
2 tomatoes, chopped
2 cloves garlic, crushed
1 tbsp dried mixed herbs
Salt and pepper

Instructions
- Heat oil in a frying pan and sweat onions and garlic.
- Add vegetables and stir occasionally until cooked.
- Serve with fresh bread or pasta.

Wild Mushroom Sauté

Serves 2

Ingredients
2 tbsps olive oil
1 clove garlic, crushed
1 small red chilli, deseeded and sliced
250g assorted mushrooms, sliced
Juice ½ lemon
1 tbsp fresh parsley, chopped
Salt and pepper

Instructions
- Heat oil in a frying pan.
- Add garlic and chilli and cook over a moderate heat for a minute.
- Add mushrooms and cook over a high heat until liquid has reduced.
- Add lemon juice and parsley.
- Season and serve with fresh bread.

Omelettes

Serves 1

Ingredients
3 eggs, beaten
1 tbsp butter
2 tbsps oil
Salt and pepper

Instructions
- Heat butter and oil in a frying pan over a high heat.
- When butter and oil begin to foam add eggs.
- Add additional ingredients and cook until egg is cooked.
- Serve.

Suggested Fillings
- Asparagus and ham
- Grated cheese
- Courgettes, capers and anchovies
- Mushrooms and a little grated truffle
- Cooked onions
- Herbs
- Tomatoes
- Spinach or swiss chard
- Leeks
- Chopped olives
- Artichoke hearts
- Red pepper, ham, tomatoes, parsley and garlic

PASTA and RICE

Basic Pasta Sauces

Fresh Tomato Sauce
1 tbsp olive oil / 1 clove garlic, crushed / 400g cherry tomatoes, halved / 2 cups fresh basil, chopped
- Put tomatoes in boiling water for 2 minutes, remove from water and peel.
- Heat oil in a large frying pan, add garlic and cook for 2 minutes over a moderate heat.
- Add cherry tomatoes and cook until it becomes a sauce. Add water or wine if it is becoming too dry.
- Add further ingredients of your choice and cook.
- Add basil.
- Add cooked pasta and stir.
- Serve with fresh parmesan.

Garlic and Chilli Sauce
3 tbsps olive oil / 2 cloves garlic, finely chopped / 1 red chilli, finely chopped / 2 tbsps fresh parsley, finely chopped
- Heat oil in a pan and cook garlic and chilli over a gentle heat until softened.
- Add further ingredients of your choice.
- Add cooked pasta and sprinkle with parsley.
- Serve with fresh parmesan.

Broad Beans and Smoked Salmon Pasta

Serves 2

Ingredients
2 cups pasta
1 tbsp olive oil
1 clove garlic, crushed
3 slices smoked salmon, chopped
2 cups broad beans, cooked
80ml cream
Handful of mint, finely chopped
Parmesan, freshly grated

Instructions
- Cook pasta.
- Heat oil in a large pan, add garlic, smoked salmon and broad beans.
- Cook over a gentle heat until garlic and salmon are cooked.
- Add mint, cream and pasta.
- Stir.
- Serve with freshly grated parmesan.

Chestnuts and Mushroom Pasta

Serves 2

Ingredients
2 tbsps butter
50g peeled chestnuts, chopped
2 cloves garlic, chopped
100g wild mushrooms or a mixture of wild and cultivated
40ml double cream
1 tbsp parsley, chopped
1 tbsp lemon juice
2 cups pasta
Salt and pepper
Parmesan, freshly grated

Instructions
- Melt 1 tbsp butter and fry chestnuts until heated through.
- Add garlic and cook for 1 minute. Set aside.
- Melt remaining butter in frying pan, add mushrooms, cook for 2 minutes.
- Add cream, parsley and lemon juice and cook until mushrooms are tender - about 3-5 minutes.
- Stir in chestnuts and season.
- Meanwhile cook pasta.
- Drain pasta and mix with chestnut sauce and sprinkle with grated parmesan.
- Serve.

Pasta with Clams

Serves 2

Ingredients
400g clams
2 cups past
2 tbsps olive oil
2 cloves garlic, thinly sliced
1 red chilli, finely chopped
1 cup dry white wine
1 handful fresh parsley, chopped
Zest ¼ lemon

Instructions
- One by one throw clams into a large bowl to dislodge sand and throw away any that do not react as they will be dead.
- Put live clams into another bowl and cover with water. Do this several times to rinse sand out of the clams.
- Cook pasta.
- Heat oil, garlic and chilli.
- Add clams to garlic and chill and cook for 30 seconds.
- Add wine and half the parsley and cook over a medium heat for about 4 minutes, stirring from time to time.
- Discard any unopened clams.
- Stir in the pasta.
- Serve with the remaining parsley and lemon zest.

Creamy Ham Pasta

Serves 2

Ingredients
2 cups past
1 tbsp olive oil
1 clove garlic, finely chopped
100g ham, chopped
2 tbsps lemon juice
½ cup cream
1 tbsp fresh parsley, finely chopped
Parmesan, freshly grated

Instructions
- Cook pasta.
- Fry garlic in butter over a gentle heat.
- Add pasta, ham, cream, parsley and lemon juice and heat through.
- Serve with freshly grated parmesan.

Pasta with Spring Vegetables

Serves 2

Ingredients
2 cups pasta
100g streaky bacon, chopped
2 cups fresh peas
2 cups fresh broad beans
2 small leeks, sliced
1 cup double cream
2 tbsp fresh mint, chopped

Instructions
- Cook vegetables in boiling water and keep warm once cooked.
- Cook pasta.
- Fry bacon until crispy.
- Add vegetables and cream.
- Drain pasta and add to frying pan.
- Add mint and stir.
- Serve.

Pasta with Artichokes and Peas

Serves 2

Ingredients
2 cups pasta
100g fresh peas in their pods, shelled
10 marinated artichokes, roughly chopped
1 tbsp olive oil
1 small shallot, finely chopped
1 clove garlic, finely chopped
Zest and juice of ½ a lemon
125ml dry white wine
1 tsp capers, finely chopped
1 tbsp fresh parsley, finely chopped
Parmesan, freshly grated

Instructions
- Cook pasta.
- Gently cook shallot and garlic in oil until softened.
- Add artichokes, lemon juice and zest, wine and capers.
- Simmer and reduce the liquid.
- Add pasta and parsley.
- Serve with freshly grated parmesan.

Seafood Pasta

Serves 2

Ingredients
2 cups pasta
1 carrot, cut into matchsticks
1 tbsp olive oil
250g uncooked shelled prawns
2 cups peas
250g scallops
1 clove garlic, crushed
2 tbsps fresh basil, chopped
1 tsp lemon rind, grated
2 tbsps lemon juice
Pepper, freshly ground

Instructions
- Cook pasta.
- Heat oil in frying pan, add prawns, carrot, peas, scallops and garlic.
- Stir fry until seafood is cooked.
- Add pasta, herbs, lemon rind, juice and pepper.
- Stir and serve.

Tomato and Chilli Pasta

Serves 2

Ingredients
2 cups pasta
1 tbsp olive oil
1 cloves garlic, crushed
½ red chilli, deseeded and finely chopped
400g cherry tomatoes, halved
20 black olives, sliced
2 cups fresh basil, chopped
Parmesan, freshly grated

Instructions
- Cook pasta.
- Heat oil in a large frying pan and add garlic and chilli.
- Cook for 2 minutes.
- Add cherry tomatoes and olives and cook for 5 minutes.
- Stir in basil.
- Add mixture to pasta and stir.
- Serve sprinkled with parmesan.

Mushroom Risotto

Serves 2

Ingredients
1 onion, sliced
1 cup risotto rice
250g mushrooms
1 cup white wine
2 cups vegetable stock
1 tsp parsley, chopped
2 tbsps parmesan, freshly grated and more to sprinkle

Instructions
- Sweat onions for about 1 minute.
- Add mushrooms and cook for another minute.
- Add risotto rice and stir before adding stock and wine in small quantities.
- Regularly stir risotto and add wine and stock in small quantities for about 20 minutes until rice is cooked.
- Stir in parmesan.
- Serve with parmesan grated and sprinkled on top of risotto.

Leek and Bacon Risotto

Serves 2

Ingredients
100g streaky bacon, chopped
4 small leeks, trimmed and finely sliced
2 cloves garlic, crushed
½ cup arborio rice
1 cup white wine
500ml vegetable stock
2 tbsps parmesan, freshly grated and more to sprinkle

Instructions
- Heat bacon in a frying pan.
- Add leeks and garlic and cook until soft.
- Add rice and stir to coat rice in fat from the bacon.
- Regularly stir risotto and add wine and stock in small quantities for about 20 minutes or until rice is cooked.
- Stir in parmesan.
- Serve with parmesan grated and sprinkled on top of risotto.

Scallop and Prawn Risotto

Serves 2

Ingredients
2 tbsps olive oil
1 shallot, finely chopped
2 cloves garlic, finely chopped
½ cup arborio rice
1 cup white wine
500ml vegetable stock
100g scallops, uncooked
100g prawns, uncooked
2 tbsps parmesan, freshly grated and more to sprinkle
Parsley

Instructions
- Heat oil in a frying pan.
- Add shallots and gently cook until soft.
- Add garlic and rice and stir, coating rice with the oil.
- Regularly stir risotto and add wine and stock in small quantities for about 20 minutes or until rice is cooked.
- After 15 minutes add scallops and prawns.
- Stir in parmesan when rice is almost cooked and scallops and prawns are fully cooked.
- Serve with freshly grated parmesan sprinkled on top of risotto.

Asparagus and Lemon Risotto

Serves 2

Ingredients
1 bunch asparagus, cut into 2cm lengths
1 tbsp olive oil
1 tsp butter
1 shallot, finely chopped
½ cup arborio rice
½ cup white wine
500ml vegetable stock
Zest and juice of ½ a lemon
2 tbsps parmesan, freshly grated and more to sprinkle

Instructions
- Cook asparagus, refresh under cold water and set aside.
- Heat oil and butter in a frying pan.
- Add shallots and gently cook until soft.
- Add rice and stir, coating rice with oil and butter.
- Regularly stir risotto and add wine and stock in small quantities for about 20 minutes or until the rice is cooked.
- A few minutes before rice is cooked add asparagus, lemon zest and juice and parmesan.
- Stir well and serve with grated parmesan.

FISH and SHELLFISH

Types of Fish

OILY FISH - herring, mackerel, salmon, trout, whitebait, eel.

These fish suit barbecuing and frying. Try dusting with a little flour and frying in a little butter and oil with some chopped garlic.

MEDITERRANEAN FISH (neither oily nor non oily) - bream, gurnard, mullet, sea bass.

Ideally cook on a barbecue or with Mediterranean ingredients like olive oil, garlic, aromatic herbs, olives and anchovies.

ROUND FISH (non oily) - Cod family - cod, haddock, hake, ling, Pollack, whiting, monkfish, john dory.

These fish can be pan fried, stir fried, steamed and barbecued.

FLAT FISH (non oily) - brill, halibut, plaice, sole, turbot.

These fish are best pan fried. Try pan frying with a little butter and oil, chopped tomato, crushed garlic, lemon juice and some fresh chopped basil.

LARGE FISH (non oily) - Skate, shar, swordfish, tuna, conger eel.

Try barbecuing steaks, making kebabs or pan frying. Marinade beforehand in olive oil, lemon juice and fresh thyme.

Mediterranean Fish

Serves 2

Ingredients
2 fish fillets - Either bream, gurnard, mullet or sea bass
2 tbsps olive oil
2 cloves garlic, finely sliced
500g cherry tomatoes, halved
2 tbsps balsamic vinegar
Handful green olives, sliced
Handful basil, chopped

Instructions
- Heat oil in frying pan and add fish fillets, skin down.
- Add garlic, tomatoes, balsamic vinegar and olives.
- When fish is cooked add basil and stir.
- Serve with fresh bread.

Sole Meuniere

Serves 2

Ingredients
½ cup butter
2 tbsps flour
Salt and pepper
4 sole fillets, skinned
Juice 1 lemon
2 tbsps parsley, chopped

Instructions
- First clarify ¼ cup butter by heating to a high temperature in the frying pan and then skimming off the scum on the top.
- Season flour with salt and pepper and place on plate. Dip fish in the seasoned flour to coat lightly and evenly.
- Heat clarified butter in a frying pan until it sizzles. Add fish and cook over a moderate heat for about 4 - 5 minutes on each side until crisp but not brown.
- Add remaining butter to pan and heat until it goes brown, add lemon juice and parsley and pour over fish.
- Serve with salad and bread or vegetables and potatoes.

Creamy Monkfish

Serves 2

Ingredients
1 tbsp butter
1 small shallot, finely chopped
150g monkfish, cut into chunks
2 slices smoked salmon, chopped
150g baby mushrooms, halved
100g prawns, raw
Juice ½ lemon
80ml dry white wine
125ml vegetable stock
40ml double cream

Instructions
- Sweat shallots until opaque.
- Add mushrooms, monkfish, smoked salmon, prawns and lemon juice and cook.
- Once cooked remove mushrooms, monkfish, smoked salmon and prawns and keep warm.
- Add wine, vegetable stock and cream. Reduce to half.
- Add mushrooms, monkfish, smoked salmon and prawns. Heat through.
- Serve with potatoes and salad or fresh bread and salad.

Sea Bass with Lemon and Capers

Serves 2

Ingredients
4 fillets sea bass
1 tbsp olive oil
1 tbsp butter
Juice of ½ lemon
2 tbsps capers
Handful parsley, chopped

Instructions
- Cook sea bass skin down in hot oil.
- Once cooked add butter, lemon juice and capers.
- Heat gently for a minute.
- Add parsley and stir.
- Serve with potatoes or bread and vegetables or salad.

Sea Bass with Fennel and Wine

Serves 2

Ingredients
4 fillets sea bass
1 bulb fennel, finely sliced
1 tbsp butter
1 cup white wine

Instructions
- Cook fennel in wine until the wine has reduced.
- Add butter and sea bass on top of fennel, skin side down and cook sea bass.
- Add water or extra wine if the fennel is becoming too dry before the fish has cooked.
- Serve sea bass on a bed of fennel with potatoes and vegetables.

Garlic Prawns

Serves 2

Ingredients
500g large raw prawns
2 tbsps olive oil
2 cloves garlic, chopped
Juice of ½ lemon
2 tbsps chopped fresh parsley

Instructions
- Wash and dry unpeeled prawns.
- Heat oil in frying pan and add garlic and fry until soft.
- Add prawns and stir fry over medium heat until cooked.
- Remove prawns and stir in lemon juice.
- Serve immediately with fresh bread.

Note
- If you prefer not to peel the prawns once served, the prawns can be substituted for 400g of defrosted raw prawns.

Peppered Prawns

Serves 2

Ingredients
400g cooked prawns
2 red peppers, sliced
1 tbsp freshly ground pepper
1 tbsp olive oil
2 cloves garlic, crushed
250ml rosé wine

Instructions
- Shell and devein prawns, leaving tails intact.
- Heat oil in frying pan, add garlic, peppers and ground pepper.
- Cook for approximately 2 minutes.
- Add wine and continue to cook until peppers are tender.
- Add prawns and cook until heated through.
- Serve with rice.

Notes
- A quicker option is to buy ready prepared frozen prawns 300g - thoroughly defrosted.

Prawns with Fennel

Serves 2

Ingredients
500g fresh raw unpeeled prawns
1 tbsp olive oil
1 small onion
1 clove garlic, crushed
1 fennel bulb, sliced
1 x 200g can of tomatoes, chopped
125ml pastis

Instructions
- Peel and devein prawns.
- Heat oil in pan, add onion, cook, stirring until onion is soft. Add garlic, fennel, tomatoes and pastis.
- Bring to the boil, reduce heat, simmer uncovered for approximately 10 minutes.
- Add prawns, cook for about 3 minutes, or until prawns change colour.
- Serve with rice.

Notes
- A quicker option is to buy ready prepared frozen prawns 300g - thoroughly defrosted.

Moules Marinieres

Serves 2

Ingredients
1 tbsp butter
2 shallots, chopped
1 clove garlic, crushed
100ml dry white wine
1 tbsp fresh parsley, chopped
1kg fresh mussels, washed and debearded
400ml double cream
Salt and pepper

Instructions
- Wash mussels under cold running water, removing any beards and discarding broken or dead mussels.
- Heat butter in a pan and sauté shallots over a medium high heat until soft.
- Add garlic, wine and half parsley to the pan and bring to the boil.
- Add mussels and reduce the heat a little.
- Cover and cook until mussels have opened.
- Discard any mussels that don't open.
- Lift mussels out and put into bowls and cover.
- Add cream to stock, season and cook for 1 - 2 minutes to heat through.
- Pour sauce over mussels and sprinkle with remaining parsley.
- Serve with fresh bread.

Mussels with Cider

Serves 2

Ingredients
2 tbsps butter
2 onions, chopped
2 cloves garlic, crushed
50 ml cider
1kg fresh mussels, de-bearded and cleaned
125ml cream
Fresh parsley to garnish.

Instructions
- Wash mussels under cold running water, removing any beards and discarding broken or dead mussels.
- Melt butter in saucepan. Add onions and cook until soft, add garlic and cook for 2 minutes.
- Stir in cider and bring to the boil.
- Add mussels. Cover and cook until mussels have opened. Remove mussels with slotted spoon and place into bowls discarding any that have not opened. Bring sauce to boil.
- Add cream and cook until reduced.
- Pour sauce over mussels and garnish with parsley.
- Serve with fresh bread.

Mussels with Leeks and Cider

Serves 2

Ingredients
1kg fresh mussels
1 tbsp olive oil
2 shallots, finely chopped
1 leek, finely chopped
1 clove garlic, finely chopped
250ml farm cider
1 tbsp double cream
Handful of fresh parsley, finely chopped

Instructions
- Wash mussels under cold running water, removing any beards and discarding broken or dead mussels.
- Gently cook shallots and leeks in a large pan with olive oil until softened.
- Add garlic and cook for 1 minute and then add cider.
- Add mussels, cover and cook for 3-4 minutes until all mussels have opened. Discard any that haven't opened.
- Stir in cream, parsley and seasoning.
- Serve with fresh bread.

Whiting with Tomato, Thyme and Pine Nuts

Serves 2

Ingredients
4 fillets whiting
Flour for dusting
250g cherry tomatoes, halved
2 tbsp toasted pine nuts
1 tsp fresh thyme
2 tbsps olive oil
Juice 1 lemon
Salt and pepper

Instructions
- Dust skin side of fish in flour.
- Gently heat olive oil in a frying pan and add whiting skin side down.
- Add tomatoes, pine nuts, thyme, lemon juice and season with salt and pepper.
- Once whiting is cooked remove from frying pan and place on plates and spoon over the tomato sauce.
- Serve with Fresh bread or potatoes and a salad.

Langoustines Provençal

Serves 2

Ingredients
1 tbsp olive oil
2 shallots, chopped
300g cherry tomatoes
2 cloves garlic, crushed
1 tsp tomato puree
750ml white wine
Bouquet garni
300g langoustines
Salt and pepper
Parsley, chopped, to garnish.

Instructions
- Heat oil in frying pan. Add shallots and cook for 1 minute.
- Add garlic and cook briefly before adding tomato puree. Heat.
- Add wine and bring to the boil and simmer until syrupy.
- Add tomatoes and bouquet garni and heat.
- Add raw langoustines. Boil until langoustines are pink and cooked.
- Sprinkle with parsley.
- Serve with fresh bread.

Monkfish with Garlic, Tomatoes and Olives

Serves 2

Ingredients
1 tbsp olive oil
300g monkfish, trimmed and cut into 5cm pieces
1 cloves garlic, crushed
3 tomatoes, peeled and chopped
4 black olives
Handful fresh basil, chopped
Salt and pepper

Instructions
- Heat oil in a frying pan and fry monkfish and garlic until fish turns opaque.
- Stir in tomatoes, olives and basic and cook for 1 - 2 minutes.
- Serve with new potatoes and vegetables or salad.

Alternative
- Replace the monkfish with king prawns or scallops.

MEAT

Peppered Steak

Serves 2

Ingredients
2 fillet steaks
2 tbsps pepper, freshly ground
1 clove garlic, crushed
2 tbsps butter
1 tbsp brandy
2 tbsps double cream

Instructions
- Press pepper and garlic into steaks.
- Heat butter in frying pan. Add steak to frying pan and cook as desired.
- Remove steak and keep warm.
- Add brandy and cream to pan and heat.
- Put steaks onto plates and pour over sauce.
- Serve with salad and fresh bread.

Creamy Chicken and Mushrooms

Serves 2

Ingredients
1 tbsp olive oil
2 chicken breasts
150g mushrooms, quartered
250ml vegetable stock
1 tbsp brandy
125ml cream
Juice ½ lemon
Salt and pepper

Instructions
- Heat oil in a frying pan and cook chicken over a moderate heat for about 10-15 minutes.
- Add mushrooms and fry for 5 minutes, stirring occasionally.
- Add stock.
- Simmer gently for about 20 minutes or until chicken is completely cooked.
- Remove chicken, cover and keep warm.
- Add brandy to the frying pan and bring to the boil and boil for 2 minutes.
- Add cream and lemon juice, and boil until the liquid is thickened.
- Season and return chicken to the frying pan and heat for about 5 minutes.
- Serve with fresh bread and salad or potatoes and vegetables.

Chicken Provençal

Serves 2

Ingredients
250g tomatoes
2 chicken breasts
1 tbsp olive oil
1 small onion, finely chopped
3 cloves garlic, crushed
1 tsp sugar
250ml rosé wine

Instructions
- Put tomatoes in boiling water for 2 minutes. Remove from water. Peel and halve.
- Heat oil in frying pan and add chicken and cook for 10 minutes.
- Add onions and sauté for 1 -2 minutes until soft.
- Add garlic and cook for 1 minute.
- Add sugar, tomatoes and wine.
- Cook for 10 minutes or until tomatoes have softened and wine has reduced.
- Make sure chicken is thoroughly cooked.
- Serve with new potatoes or bread and salad.

Lamb with Thyme and Garlic

Serves 2

Ingredients
4 lamb cutlets
1 tbsp fresh thyme, chopped
2 tbsps olive oil
8 cloves garlic
4 tbsps butter
Salt and pepper

Instructions
- Rub thyme into cutlets.
- Heat oil and 2 tbsps butter in a frying pan. Once very hot, add lamb and cook quickly until brown on both sides.
- Lower the heat.
- Season lamb and add remaining butter. When it begins to sizzle add garlic and cook until soft and brown.
- Place lamb on plates and pour over the juices.
- Serve with potatoes and vegetables or salad and fresh bread.

DESSERTS

Melon with Sweet Wine

Serves 2

Ingredients
1 Cavaillon or Galia melon
Sweet white wine like a Sauternes

Instructions
- Cut melon in half and remove the seeds.
- Pour in a generous amount of chilled wine.
- Serve.

Chestnuts in Wine

Serves 2

Ingredients
200g chestnuts
1 x 5cm long ribbon orange zest
200ml Sauternes wine
75ml red wine
2 tbsps sugar
Ice cream or double cream to serve

Instructions
- Put chestnuts, orange zest, Sauternes, red wine and sugar in pan.
- Bring to the boil and simmer gently until wine has reduced to a thick syrup – approximately 30 minutes.
- Put into bowls.
- Serve with ice cream or double cream.

Pancakes

Ingredients
3 eggs
1 cup flour
500ml milk
Butter for frying

Makes approximately 12 small light French style pancakes.

Instructions
- Mix flour and eggs and add milk slowly to avoid lumps.
- Rest for ½ hour.
- Melt 1 tbsp butter in frying pan and mix melted butter into mixture.
- Pour just enough pancake mixture into frying pan and cook on both sides.
- Add filling and serve.
- Do the same for the rest of the pancake.

Suggested Fillings for Pancakes
- Butter/sugar – a little melted butter sprinkled with sugar.
- Sweetened chestnut cream.
- Butter sprinkled with powdered drinking chocolate.
- Caramel.
- Apples – ½ apple, ½ tbsp demerara sugar, ½ tbsp butter, ½ tbsp brandy.
- Oranges – segments of 1 orange. Put into pan with 1 tbsps sugar and 1 tbsps Cointreau - Heat until sugar has dissolved and liquid has become syrupy.

Fruit Salad

Serves 2

Ingredients
½ cup sugar
½ cup water
100ml red wine
1 peach, sliced
1 apricot, sliced
½ orange peel
60g raspberries
60g redcurrant
60g cherries
1 tbsp brandy

Instructions
- Mix sugar, water and wine in saucepan and heat until syrupy. Leave to cool.
- Prepare fruit and put into bowls.
- Pour over syrup and brandy.
- Serve with ice cream.

Peaches in Brandy

Serves 2

Ingredients
⅓ cup brandy
1 tbsp sugar
2 peaches
Double cream to serve

Instructions
- Place peaches in boiling water for a couple of minutes to loosen the skins.
- Peel peaches and remove stone and cut into quarters.
- Place peaches, brandy and sugar in a bowl.
- Leave for a couple of hours in a fridge.
- Serve with double cream.

Poached Peaches and Apricots

Serves 2

Ingredients
2 tbsps sugar
360ml dry white wine
2 strawberries
4 peaches, peeled
4 apricots, peeled
Double cream to serve

Instructions
- Put sugar and wine in a saucepan and heat gently until sugar has dissolved.
- Bring to the boil and cook for 3 - 4 minutes.
- Add fruit and boil for 6 - 7 minutes or until peaches are soft.
- Remove fruit and boil until liquid has become a syrup.
- Put into bowls and pour over with sauce.
- Serve with double cream.

Notes
- To peel peaches and apricots, put whole fruit into a bowl of boiling water. Leave for 1 - 2 minutes then drain. The skins should then peel away easily.
- If fruit is not quite ripe simmer gently in a little sugar and water solution for about 6 - 8 minutes or until just tender. Drain and peel.

Figs with Honey and Marsala

Serves 2

Instructions

6 figs
4 tbsps honey
Juice ½ lemon
2 tbsps Marsala or other sweet wine
1 tsp fresh thyme

Instructions

- Place figs in the bottom of a pan and add honey, lemon, Marsala and thyme.
- Cover and cook for 20 minutes over a low heat.
- Add more wine if starting to boil dry.
- Serve with ice cream.

Plums in Red Wine

Serves 2

Ingredients
4 large plums
8 tbsps sugar
150ml red wine
Zest of 1 lemon, grated
½ bay leaf
1 clove
Double cream to serve

Instructions
- Place all the ingredients in a pan.
- Bring to the boil and simmer until plums are soft.
- Remove plums and put into bowls.
- Boil liquid until it becomes a syrup.
- Serve with double cream or ice cream.

Poached Pears in Espresso Syrup

Serves 2

Ingredients
2 pears, peeled and stalk remaining
¾ cup espresso or strong fresh black coffee
1 cup sugar
3 cardamom pods, crushed
Juice and grated zest of ½ lemon
Water

Instructions
- Cut a little off the base of each pear to keep them upright.
- Put ingredients except pears in a saucepan and bring to the boil and stir until sugar has dissolved.
- Add pears, bring to the boil. Cover, reduce heat.
- Simmer for 20-25 minutes or until pears are tender.
- Remove pears and put into a bowls.
- Boil syrup rapidly until syrupy.
- Serve with double cream or ice cream.

APPENDIX

Store Cupboard Essentials

To take:

- Capers
- Extra virgin olive oil
- Balsamic vinegar
- Dijon mustard
- Flour
- Sugar
- Sea salt
- Pine nuts
- Vegetable stock cubes
- Pepper mill
- Garlic
- Honey
- Rice
- Risotto Rice
- Pasta
- Couscous
- Quinoa
- Tinned tomatoes
- Tinned artichokes
- Tinned anchovies
- Bottled green olives

Growing Herbs:
Parsley / Basil / Mint / Thyme

Measurements

¼ cup of rice per person
1 cup of pasta per person
¼ cup of couscous per person
¼ cup of quinoa per person

1ml - millilitre
1cl - centilitre = 10ml
1lt - litre = 1000ml

60ml = ¼ cup
80ml = ⅓ cup
125ml = ½ cup
250ml = 1 cup

Picnics

In addition to sandwiches and salads here are some picnic ideas which can be sourced either from the market and local shops:

From the supermarket:
- Breadsticks
- Juice cartons and bottles of water
- Crisps
- Rotiserie chicken

From the delicatessen:
- Patés
- Sliced cured sausages
- Sliced hams
- Local cheeses
- Olives
- Artichoke hearts
- Sundried tomatoes
- Tapenade
- Hummus
- Taramasalata

From the local baker:
- Speciality bread
- Bread rolls

From the market:
- Baby tomatoes
- Fruit including: bananas, apples, apricots, strawberries, pears, plums, peaches etc

Sandwiches

Sandwich Ideas
Here are some ideas for sandwiches. Some obvious but easily forgotten and other ones to tempt the taste buds:

Cheese and Tomato / Smoked Salmon and Cream Cheese / Tomato / Ham and Cheese / Cucumber / Radish / Egg and Cress / Egg and Rocket / Avocado and Prawn Mayonnaise / Avocado, Rocket and Lime Mayonnaise

Tuna Baguette
1 baguette
1 tin tuna, drained
1 tbsp capers
Handful rocket
2 tbsps mayonnaise

Baguette with Asparagus and Ham
1 baguette
8 spears of asparagus, cooked
8 slices of Ham

Baguette with Aubergine, Ham and Olives
1 baguette
1 aubergine, fried in olive oil
8 slices ham
8 large green olives, finely sliced

Barbecue

Honey and Lemon Marinade for Beef
1 tsp honey
2 tbsps lemon juice
2 cloves garlic, crushed

Brandy Marinade
2 tbsps brandy
1 tbsp honey
1 clove garlic, crushed

Salsa
4 tomatoes, finely chopped
1 small red onion, finely chopped
1 clove garlic, crushed
½ red chilli, finely chopped
Juice of 1 lime
1 tbsp olive oil

Olive and Cucumber Relish
20ml olive oil
50g pitted green olives, chopped
Juice 1 lemon
¼ cucumber, peeled, seeded and diced
1 small chilli, finely chopped
Handful parsley, chopped

Food Pairings

Here is a basic list of foods that work well together.

Anchovy - capers, lemon.

Artichokes - olive oil, lemon, thyme, garlic.

Aubergines - olive oil, garlic, courgettes.

Avocados - lime, chilli.

Beetroot - watercress, walnuts, orange.

Celery - apple, blue cheese, chestnuts.

Courgettes - garlic, olive oil, herbs, tomatoes.

Cucumber - mint, yoghurt.

Fennel - pork, olives.

Figs - cured ham.

Goats cheese - smoked salmon, capers.

Mushrooms - chestnuts, truffles.

Peaches - mango.

Peppers - basil, olive oil, tomatoes, anchovies, garlic.

Tomatoes - basil, garlic, avocado.

Strawberry - peaches.

About the Author

Liz Garnett has been a travel photographer for over 27 years. In that time she has concentrated on photographing France and her home county of Kent in southern England. Her images have sold worldwide and been reproduced in magazines, newspapers and books.

In 2012 she published the first in a series of French Holiday Cookery books for English speaking holidaymakers travelling to France on camping or self-catering holidays. The recipes require no more than two gas burners and are designed to be hassle-free and utilise fresh local produce. Ingredients are translated into French and the books include a French/English glossary of ingredients. British Holiday Cookery has been developed on the back of the French Holiday Cookery series especially for camping and self-catering holiday makers in the United Kingdom.

In 2020, Liz published her first novel, Journey, about an artist who follows the Tro Breiz pilgrimage route around Brittany, France.

Liz continues to take photographs and write and further details on her current projects can be found on her website:

www.lizgarnett.com

www.ingramcontent.com/pod-product-compliance
Lightning Source LLC
LaVergne TN
LVHW021541080426
835509LV00019B/2762